A ROMANCE

OF

ARLINGTON HOUSE

BY

SARAH A. REED

THE CHAPPLE PUBLISHING CO., LTD.

BOSTON, MASS.

[1908]

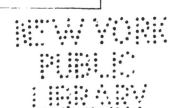

Copyright, 1908

CHAPPLE PUBLISHING COMPANY, LTD.

BOSTON

Dedicated to

MY STUDY CLASSES

IN GRATEFUL MEMORY OF THE

MANY PLEASANT HOURS

WE HAVE SPENT TOGETHER

Lovingly your own
Virginia.

THE PROLOGUE

THIS little prologue is not written as an apology for the publication of these old letters, but because the letters themselves have a history that may perchance enhance their interest. The letters were written at Arlington in eighteen hundred and twenty-four, and therefore are closely associated with the beautiful old place that is now one of the sights of Washington.

I first saw Arlington House in the early seventies, when it was simply a dismantled and deserted home; for it was not then easy of access, and its associations were too intensely sad to attract those in search of diversion.

The sunshine and beauty of a May morning had tempted me to accept the invitation of the army officer at whose home I was a guest, to occupy the seat beside him in the light one-seated buggy that stood at his door ready for a trip to Arlington, which for him was in the line of official duty.

My friend had served all through the war, whose sorrowful memories were, at that near date, so vivid and personal. And as we drove along he told me much about the condition of Washington during those hard years between sixty-one and sixty-five.

I knew little or nothing about Arlington, and listened with much interest to his account of a visit he had made to the mansion soon after it had been abandoned by the Lee family. The grounds of the great estate soon became a camping-place for the Union army, and a temporary hospital was erected near the entrance; and Arlington soon became a favorite drive for President Lincoln when he wished to escape from the turmoil that always beset him at the White House.

My friend told me that the President often spent an hour or two walking alone up and down the grand porch that overlooks the river. One can imagine what conflicts between hope and fear were fought out in the secret of his own thoughts as he walked and meditated, quieted and soothed by the beautiful views that met his eyes whenever he lifted them to look across the sloping lawn, down to the wide river and the hillsides beyond.

One day Mr. Lincoln's quiet meditations were broken in upon by General Meigs, who was then in charge of the hospitals about Washington. Standing beside the President, Meigs began to talk of his own close intimacy with Robert E. Lee, when they had been officers together in the army that Lee had forsaken. He said: "I loved him as a brother, but I can never forgive him for being against instead of with us now; and whatever the issue of this war, he should never again enjoy this estate. I am just now in great perplexity as to where to bury our dead. Let us settle forever the question as to whom this land shall belong, by making it a resting-place for the Union dead."

Mr. Lincoln hesitated, looked out over the beautiful grounds and up at the stately mansion, and shook his head.

"Why not?" said Meigs. "Is any place too good for the men who have given up home and all to fight that the Union may be sustained?"

As Mr. Lincoln turned away, without having granted General Meigs' request, he saw, standing near, a squad of men in charge of the bodies of a number of soldiers who had just died in the hospital. The sight touched his heart, and turning abruptly, he said: "Do as you wish."

General Meigs at once ordered the graves to be dug on the sloping lawn. And so was inaugurated the Soldiers' Cemetery at Arlington, where sleep now "Beneath the low green tent, whose curtain never outward swings," so many of our nation's heroes.

While my friend had been giving me these reminiscences of Arlington, he had driven swiftly out of Washington, along the rough streets of Georgetown, and came out upon the aqueduct across the river.

[8]

"But beyond is Arlington House. Isn't it unrivaled for beauty of situation? George Washington Custis was an artist, and he certainly chose the finest point on all his vast estate for his grand mansion. He was very proud of the house, which was modeled after the ancient temple of Theseus at Athens; and in Mr. Custis' day it was the mansion par excellence in all this part of the country."

"Yes," I said, "and I think the estate ought to have been kept for his descendants, and not desecrated by being made a burial place."

"Desecrated!" said my friend, turning to give me a piercing glance from his deep-set gray eyes. "Why, I might think I had a Southern woman beside me. How can you, a loyal Unionist, call ground desecrated because it holds the sacred dust of men who gave their lives that you might have a country that is fast becoming one of the foremost nations of the world?"

I blushingly accepted the reproof, but said that I was moved by sympathy with the Lees.

"Yes," said my friend, "that is sentiment; but from my point of view, there is justice in this place belonging to the nation. The place was bought in by the government when it was sold for delinquent taxes; but after the war the claim of the Lee family was recognized, and the appraised value paid to them. I used to go to Arlington when I was a boy, and the one thing I remember about George Washington Custis was his intense love of his country—a love that had been planted in his heart and fostered there by his adopted father, whom we all delight to name as 'The Father of His Country;' and I verily believe that Mr. Custis would rather the home he was so proud of should be national property, than to have it in the hands that had borne arms against his country, even though they were those of his own grandchildren.

"But here we are at Arlington. Let us forget the question of right and wrong, and enjoy this lovely drive."

Lovely indeed is the road that winds under

the shadow of great trees and through deep
ravines, until it emerges from the natural forest
into the lawns and gardens that surround the
house. But trees, grand old oaks, stand all about
the house, while a great level terrace, in front and
overlooking the river, opens out a panorama of
surpassing beauty. We stood for a few moments, charmed into silence by the magnificent
view that took in the city, with the great dome
of the Capitol, and the glistening whiteness of
the President's mansion, while rising above it all,
clear-cut against the blue sky, gleamed the great
white column that stands as a perpetual reminder of him whom a grateful nation still delights to name as "first in the hearts of his
countrymen." The broad Potomac, cutting its
way through the hills, opens a far-extended
view, even giving a glimpse of the old city of
Alexandria.

Seeing how absorbed I was in the charming
landscape, Colonel Benton said: "I will leave
you here for an hour or more, while I attend

to my business. You will find the door of the house open, and, if you choose, you can go within and meditate on the wrongs of the Lee family;" and with this parting thrust at my loyalty, he left me.

I stood for some time enjoying the picturesque and varied beauty of the scene, but when I turned from the enticing landscape, I found plenty to admire in the grand old mansion. The tall, massive columns of the portico would attract anyone's attention, and must have excited wonder in the early days of the Nineteenth Century, when so few people had an opportunity to look upon such a perfect reproduction of Greek architecture.

As I walked across the broad marble pavement of this portico, I thought of Mr. Lincoln, and of the sharp, stern contrast his life, with its crude, bare childhood and youth of toil and deprivation, presented to that of the man who had built, lived and died in this stately mansion. But the contrast does not stop here; for he is today remembered as a gentle, kindly gentleman, but one who made little use of the splendid opportunities afforded him, and simply drifted on with the current; while the other man, rough-hewn by the force and stress of a life of toil and hardness, stood like a great rock boulder in the pathway of disunion, and is today honored by the reverent affection of a grateful people—one whose name will go down into far-remote history as the savior of his country.

I neither met nor saw anyone as I walked for a few moments up and down the great portico, and when I stepped within the broad hall, I met only quiet and solitude. The large lofty-ceiled rooms had scarcely an article of furniture in them. The only things I found interesting to look at were several large pictures—battle scenes; and in each one General Washington was the central and conspicuous figure. I had heard that Mr. Custis was something of an artist, and so I realized that even this deserted home held some of his work, left doubtless because the pictures were a part of the walls on which they had been painted.

As I stood there alone, I pictured to myself the now bare rooms as they must have looked when filled with the handsome furniture of the olden days, and the whole house full of life and comfort. Many illustrious men and women had walked about on the floors that now gave back a doleful echo to my solitary footsteps.

I was tempted to go out into the sunshine, to escape the ghosts of memory that haunted the old house, but the broad stairway at the end of the hall seemed to invite further explorations; so I passed up to a wide, roomy upper hall, only to find all the doors that opened into it locked but one, and that admitted me into a small room above the front door. It had evidently been used as a writing-room. The broad window-seat gave one a place to sit and look out over the glorious landscape.

An empty book-case and writing-desk were a

part of the room, built in, so that they could not be removed. Still, there was so little to interest me that I decided that I would rather await my friend's return out on the lawn. As I turned away from the window, I heard the sound of footsteps in the hall below, and so knew that I was no longer the sole inmate of Arlington House. I had noticed on my way up stairs, that the stairway was decorated with a hunting scene, and, as I supposed it to be another of Mr. Custis's pictures, I stopped on the second landing to give it a more careful inspection.

As I stood with my back toward the lower stairs, I took a step backward in order to get a better view of the picture, and in doing so brought my back against a lady, who, like myse'f, had stopped on the landing to look up at the hunting scene. My movement had been so sudden and unexpected, that it threw me into her arms, which she had outstretched to save herself from a downfall. It was a rather embarrassing situation, but my apologies were received so graciously that I soon felt quite at ease, with my chance acquaintance, and, as we walked out on the lawn together, Mrs. Burke told me that she was a long-time resident of Washington, and that she had often been at Arlington when it was the beautiful and hospitable home of Robert E. Lee and his charming wife, who had made it one of the most delightful homes in or near Washington.

Then she said: "I came here today in search of what, for a better term, I may call an old landmark; and yet that does not quite express my meaning. I have been reading over some old letters that I have just discovered in a secret compartment of an old desk that once belonged to my grandmother. These letters were written at Arlington, away back in the twenties. They tell of various men and women prominent in the history of our country, but their especial interest is in the account they give of a visit of General Lafayette to Mr. Custis. Then, too, between the lines at first, and

GENERAL LAFAYETTE

From an original painting by Chappel
made shortly after his visit at
Arlington House

From an original painting by Cl ppel

openly at a later date, I found a sweet little love story; and the love story part has brought me all the way to Arlington this morning; for I want to find if there still remains on one of the window-panes of the little room above the front door a mark placed there over fifty years ago. Will you go up stairs and help me in my search?"

You may be sure I was nothing loath, and on one of the little diamond-shaped panes we found a delicately-traced picture of two rings interlocked, and each marked with a tiny initial.

"There it is," said Mrs. Burke, "just as it is described in the old letters. How remarkable that it should have remained there through all the vicissitudes that have passed over this house."

Of course I at once expressed my interest in the old letters, with their glimpses into by-gone days, to which was added the interest of a romance. And so effective was my curiosity upon the kindly nature of my newly found friend that it resulted in a call from her the very next day, and an invitation to spend a morning in her home, listening to the reading of the letters from Arlington.

My story would grow too long if I were to yield to my inclinations and tell you still more of this delightful chance acquaintance of mine, and of all that we came to be to each other in the years that followed our first meeting on the stairway at Arlington; but now we are only concerned in the fulfillment of her promise about the letters.

When I went by appointment to her lovely home on I street, I found her awaiting my arrival. First of all, she led me to the old desk that had so long been the repository of the letters, saying: "One seldom sees, nowadays, anything so quaint and beautiful as my grandmother's desk." And the desk fully justified her praise; for besides the quaint and peculiar beauty of its form and the beautiful inlaid work that covered it both within and without, the woods had a finish that only long years of care can give.

When I had admired the desk to my friend's full satisfaction, she said: "Now you may try to find the secret compartment, and if you succeed, you will have proved yourself a far better discoverer than I; for, although I knew that there was a secret compartment, I have only recently, and then quite by accident, discovered it."

It is hardly needful to say that, although I looked over and touched every part of the desk, I quite failed to find the secret so carefully guarded. Then my friend laid a finger on an innocent-looking little panel of inlaid wood, and under her touch it folded itself back and revealed an inner compartment closely packed with letters.

As Mrs. Burke handed me a package, she said: "Will you look and see how wonderfully they are preserved? I think it is, in fact, due to the honest ink and paper used in those olden days."

The packages were marked in a fine, clear handwriting: "My daughter Virginia's letters from Arlington."

We took the packages into the sunlight of the deep window that filled the front of the room, and for an hour or more 1 listened to the reading of letters then more than fifty years old, with as intense and eager an interest as if they had come from some near and dear friend. Now and then, Mrs. Burke paused in her reading to help out the story they told with facts that had come down to her family in tradition.

When the last letter had been read, and the last explanation given, I drew a deep sigh of satisfaction and said, "What would I give to have those old letters."

"Nothing you could do or give would bring to you these letters," said my friend. "But why do you want them? Is it not enough to have heard them read?"

"No," I said, "for if I had them, I could weave out of them such an interesting story of the olden times."

My friend sat very quietly for a few moments, and then she said: "Strangely enough, I have had the same thought about these letters. I believe they would interest many people. I have a perfect right to give you copies of them to use in the way you wish, for they are mine, not alone by the right of discovery, but also because I am nearest of living kin to her who wrote them; but if I give them to you, it will have to be under a sacred promise not to use them until certain conditions have been fulfilled, and it may be years before you could use them.

The promise was given, and has been faithfully kept. In due time the copies came into my possession, and found in my desk a seclusion as inviolate as that of the old desk in which the originals so long reposed. But now the restriction has been removed, and Virginia Colton's letters, written eighty-one years ago, are free to seek a wider circulation.

I

Arlington, October 2, 1824.

Dear Mother—As Cæsar is to carry this letter
to you, I much fear that, in spite of his promise to
hold his tongue until you have read it, he will,
true to that garrulous nature of his, have given
you his own highly-colored story of our adventures before you have read the account I am
about to write for the edification of the dear
home circle at Wyndham Manor.

Lest the roll of Cæsar's eyes, and his many
and mysterious exclamations, may have unduly
alarmed you, I make haste to bid you remember that "All is well that ends well," and I am
here under dear, kind cousin Mary's care, not
one whit the worse for the accident that befell
us yesterday afternoon.

We spent the night of our first day from
home at Uncle John's, and took an early start
for Arlington yesterday. Such a lovely ride as

we had through the woods, the grand old trees
arching over the road most of the way, and
wild flowers and ferns fairly brushing against the
carriage.

I longed to have you with me, for I·know
how you would have enjoyed it all. Chrissie
got her share of pleasure out of it, and every
now and then I made Cæsar stop, so that Chrissie and I could walk a little way and gather
some of the flowers. We had a nice lunch, that
we ate under the trees beside a wayside spring,
while the horses rested and had their noon
meal.

We found the road rather rough, but in spite
of the swinging and jolting of the carriage, I fell
into a doze, following the example of Chrissie,
whose black head had found an uncertain and
uneasy resting-place on the side of the carriage,
when we were suddenly aroused by finding ourselves in a confused heap—Chrissie on top, and
I against the carriage window. My first waking
sensation was feeling the warm blood on my

cheeks from a cut on my forehead, and we were shaken up and down by the plunging of the horses; but it was soon over, for our good horses obeyed Cæsar's frightened calls, and the carriage stopped, half-righting itself as it came to a standstill.

Cæsar managed, by dint of much pulling, to get the carriage door open, and then poor dilapidated Chrissie and I crawled out. We soon found that the only serious harm was to the carriage, which lay on its side, one wheel fast in a deep rut, and the axletree broken. We were in the midst of a dense forest, a long way from Colonel Dean's, where we had stopped to water the horses. Cæsar looked at me in a dazed way, while Chrissie wrung her hands and wailed in true darkey fashion. So I had, as father would say, to rise to meet the situation.

It was well on in the afternoon, and I judged that we must still be some distance from Arlington. We could not spend the night in that lonely place, so I sent Cæsar into the woods to find a

pole to pry the carriage out of the rut. As I
stood considering what we were to do, Cæsar
called from the woods, with quite a joyful ring
in his voice: "Miss Virginia, I think I hear a
horse coming up the road;" and looking up,
I saw not one but two horsemen on the brow of
the hill, at the foot of which our dilapidated
carriage blocked the way.

They evidently saw us at the same moment,
and, quickening the speed of their horses, were
soon beside us. One was an army officer, as I
could see by his uniform, and the other his black
servant. The young gentleman at once sprang
from his horse, and, handing the bridle to his
servant, came forward, cap in hand, saying: "I
am Captain Worthington, of the United States
army. It is a part of my commission to protect
and defend her citizens. I seem to see a case
in hand."

The captain looked so handsome as he stood
making his little speech, that — would you believe it, mother dear?—my first thought was not

of the carriage, but of my own appearance, with the blood stains on my face and my hair falling down my back. But Cæsar, who had run from the woods, was ready, in his own voluble way, to tell the tale of our misfortune.

I interrupted him to ask how near we were to Washington, or rather, Arlington; at which remark, the captain's face lighted up, and he said: "Can it be you are the Cousin Virginia that Mrs. Custis is expecting? I, too, am on my way to Arlington, and we must devise a safe conduct for you and your maid." But looking at the carriage as he spoke, he said: "I doubt if you can get there in this vehicle." Well, I can't go into details, but after what Captain Worthington called "a council of war" with the two men servants, it was decided that his man Peter should stay with Cæsar and look after the carriage and horses, while Chrissie and I rode Peter's horse, following Captain Worthington as our guide to Arlington.

We had to go rather slowly, and it was eight

o'clock in the evening before we saw glimmer-
ing lights in the distance, and Captain Worthington gave the delightful information that we
were nearing Arlington. I wondered to myself if
he was as glad to be relieved of his self-assumed
position as rescuer and guide, as I was over the
prospect of a welcome from dear Cousin Mary.

You can easily imagine the commotion our
arrival occasioned; how many questions were
asked and answered. I talked on rapidly and
excitedly, until I suddenly became aware that
Captain Worthington was letting me do all the
talking, only watching me with a merry twinkle
in his eyes; so I stopped short, and complained
of being tired, whereat Cousin Mary sent us off
to our rooms, and when we met again at the
dinner that had been long delayed by our late
arrival, I simply made the captain tell the story
of our adventures.

Well, Cæsar is here now, and the carriage
will be repaired so that he can start for home
tomorrow; he will be the bearer of this long

letter, and I will write again in a day or two. What a great, grand house this is, and so full of interesting things! I shall have so much to write about. And just to think that I am to be here with General Lafayette and his son!

Did I tell you that Captain Worthington is very handsome? But he is not young. Cousin Mary says that he must be nearly thirty years of age. You and father must write and thank him for his kindness to your ship - wrecked, or rather, carriage - wrecked, daughter. And don't forget to invite him to Wyndham. That is the least that you can do to show your gratitude that I did not perish alone in the wilderness.

The little Mary, as we have always called her, is little no longer, and she is a beautiful girl.

Well, this letter must come to an end, but not until I tell you that I learned last night why Captain Worthington is a guest at Arlington. He has been appointed aide to General Lafayette while he is in this country, and he is here making arrangements for the General's visit; and he and Mr. Custis go to Baltimore day after tomorrow, to meet the General and his party and escort them to Washington. Only the General and his son, George Washington, are to be guests at this house; the others stay in Washington.

I am going out horseback riding this afternoon. Mr. Custis has promised to show me over the plantation. He wants me to see his wonderful sheep and the famous Custis spring. I hope Captain Worthington can go with us.

Cousin Mary sends love, and says to tell you that you are going to miss the event of a life-time in not being here during General Lafayette's visit. That makes me realize how unselfish you were to send me in your place. But, oh! how I shall enjoy every moment, and you shall have full accounts. Love to Pater and my little brothers, and all the servants, especially dear old Mammy. Tell her that Chrissie does credit to her training, and she, too, is having no end of enjoyment.   Lovingly, your own

VIRGINIA.

[32]

"I am Captain Worthington of the United States army. It is part of my commission to protect and defend her citizens. I seem to see a case in hand."

II

Arlington, October 5, 1824.

Well, mother dear, I wish you were here in this cosy writing-room. You will remember that it is at the end of the second-story great hall. There is so much to tell that my pen can never jot it all down.

We have just seen Mr. Custis and Captain Worthington off for Baltimore, and Cousin Mary has had her hands full getting the house ready for her distinguished guest. Mary, the second, is busy with her lessons; so your daughter is left to her own devices, and what better can I do than tell you what has happened since my first letter started homeward.

Yesterday the weather was just perfect, and that suited our plans wonderfully well, for Mr. Custis had proposed the night before that Captain Worthington should be my companion on a horseback excursion through the park and over to the

old mansion that was the home before Mr. Custis
built this grand house. We made an early start,
and had a glorious ride. The Captain is most
gallant and charming. You would never believe
that he was not Southern-born. But he tells
me that he is a New Englander — born in Boston. I told him all about Wyndham and you
dear people this morning, and he seemed very
much interested. Then he said that he had only
faint, shadowy memories of his father and mother.
Both had died when he was very young, and he
had been adopted by his mother's brother and
had taken his uncle's name.

Did I tell you how tall and handsome he is
—a typical soldier, devoted to his profession?
You should see the gallant attention he shows
Cousin Mary. I can see that he has quite won
the heart of Mr. Custis. A soldier always sug-
gests to him the dear grandfather he so delights
to talk about. Indeed, the Captain is in high favor
with all the family, and Cousin Mary has invited
him to stay here all the time of General Lafay-

[34]

ette's visit. She argues, and quite rightly, too, that Captain Worthington ought to be near the General, and not over in Washington.

It will be nice to have him here; don't you think so? But, there, I forgot that you are in Wyndham, and can't judge what is best for Arlington; only this seems to be what father calls "a self-evident truth."

But how I am running on about other things, instead of telling you about the lovely winding road under the grand old trees. One could ride for hours just around Arlington plantation, for there are hundreds and hundreds of acres, and so much of it unbroken forest.

We did ride longer than we intended, and Mr. Custis told us that he had been waiting for us for over an hour. But he wasn't one bit cross, and was as good-natured and kind as if we had arrived on the very minute. I ran up stairs, and had my riding-habit off in no time, and joined the gentlemen as they started off on foot for the spring Mr. Custis is so proud of.

It is on the hillside, near the river, and there
is a great flow of clear cold water. Mr. Custis
has built a large pavilion near the spring, and
placed seats on the ground under the great trees,
so that it is a most attractive spot. And, only
think, everybody, high and low alike, is free to
come there and spend the day.

Cousin Mary says that Mr. Custis is always
going down to welcome and visit with the people who come to picnic at his spring-house, and
he thinks nothing of supplying all deficiencies
from his pantry.

Hospitality is surely his crowning virtue. He
says that he learned it all at Mount Vernon, where
General Washington (grandfather as he always
calls him) was ever as polite and cordial to a
poor wayfarer as to his most aristocratic guest.

I shall know all about the great Washington
soon, for he is constantly referred to and quoted.
From the spring-house we went across the beautiful fields, to look at a flock of Merino sheep.
These sheep are, next to Washington, Mr. Custis's

special hobby. He thinks that he has started
a movement that will make America the great
wool-growing country of the world, and that,
in time, we shall manufacture better wool goods
than can be produced in any part of the Old
World.

He was most enthusiastic on the subject, but
he directed all his conversation to Captain Worthington, doubtless considering it beyond me. He
talked so long that we were late for lunch; and
right after lunch Captain Worthington left for
Washington, where he had an official appointment with President Monroe.

As I had spoken to Mr. Custis of my interest in the many fine portraits that hang on the
walls of all the rooms, he offered, right after dinner last evening, to show them to me, with quite
a number of miniatures that he keeps in a quaint
old cabinet that he inherited from his Grandmother Washington.

Captain Worthington returned in time for
dinner, and such an interesting evening as we

(that "we" stands for Captain Worthington and your daughter Virginia) spent, looking on the pictured faces of so many Parkes, Custises and Washingtons. I fear that they are somewhat mixed in my mind; but, anyway, I enjoyed it all, and I am sure it made Mr. Custis happy to discourse about his ancestors. He is especially proud of a very old portrait of a certain Colonel Daniel Parke who is pictured in a rich court dress of velvet and lace, and Mr. Custis wanted us to notice that this old Daniel wore on his breast a medallion portrait of Queen Anne, which, family tradition said, had been presented to him by the good queen herself.

Then there was a John Custis and a John Parke Custice. The latter was really our Mr. Custis' grandfather; although in his talk he quite ignores his grandmother's first marriage; and grandfather with him always refers to General Washington.

He has a number of fine portraits of the General, one painted by Peale, and another by

Sharpless, also several medallions of Washington's head done on copper. One had the heads of Washington and Lafayette side by side.

With each picture of Washington hung always one of his wife, so that one can hardly help feeling that there were many George and Martha Washingtons.

There is one miniature of Mrs. Washington, painted by Robertson, when she was the first lady of the land. It is very beautiful, and is Mr. Custis' special pride, although I think he is pleased and gratified when visitors admire his own paintings. They are all battle scenes, and always with General Washington in the foreground. There are three of them, and he has told me just what battles they represent; but I only remember that one was the surrender of the British at Yorktown. They are great big pictures, and rather overwhelm one. But, mind, I did not tell that to Mr. Custis.

There is a lovely picture of Mr. Custis's sister Nellie, and one of our expected guest, George

Washington Lafayette. Mr. Custis seems especially delighted that he is to have a visit from this son of General Lafayette, for they have always kept up a correspondence since they were boys together at Mount Vernon.

I did not know anything about this son of General Lafayette's being in Washington's family for so long. It seems, he was sent to the United States when his father and mother were in prison, during those terrible days of the French Revolution, so for a time Washington had his two namesakes under his own roof.

But while I am telling you about family portraits, I must not forget the most treasured of them all, which is a miniature of General Washington painted on ivory. Mr. Custis said that his grandmother always wore it, and that after the General's death she would sit for hours looking intently at it. She had it in her hand when she died, and he values it so highly that it is kept in a cabinet in his own room.

As Mr. Custis walked about with us from

room to room, displaying his art treasures, he told us so much about his early life at Mount Vernon. He was just eight years old when Washington was made President, but he remembers all about the journey from Mount Vernon to New York, and he could tell so much about the life in New York and Philadelphia.

These remimiscences interested Captain Worthington even more than they did me: for I must own that I was not sorry when Mr. Custis was called out of the room, and I had a chance to question the Captain about his visit to the President. He said that he wished I could have seen the White House, and perhaps called upon Mrs. Monroe. He said that I must surely be in Washington to witness the arrival of General Lafayette and his party. This I know Cousin Mary has arranged for. Won't it be fine? I can hardly believe that I am to go and do and see so much, and I am as happy as a bird.

By the way, that reminds me to tell you that Captain Worthington asked me to sing for him, and we spent two hours alone together, quite absorbed in music. I played on Cousin Mary's harpsichord. The Captain has a fine tenor voice, and we sang song after song, until (I am ashamed to tell you) Cousin Mary had to come in and warn us that it was nearly midnight, and the breakfast hour had been set early for the next morning, on account of the travelers needing all the daylight for their long journey on horseback. Cousin Mary said that I need not come down for the early breakfast, but I would not have missed it for anything. Indeed I was down in such good time that the Captain and I had a walk to the spring before the breakfast bell rang. And what do you think he said as we came back? Why, that he would miss me every hour he was away. Only think of your little girl being of enough importance to be missed by an officer of the United States army!

But that was just a polite speech. Doubtless he will not think of me twice while he is away. He will be all taken up with the grand folks he will be with. Cousin Mary says that it is a great honor for him to have this position of aide to General Lafayette, and that it was given him as a reward for his skill and bravery in the war with the Indians.

Well, they got off, as I have already told you, in good time this morning. And now, before I close my letter, I will go and see if 'Cousin Mary has any message to send you.

Later.—It is two hours since I laid down my pen, but I found that I could help Cousin Mary, and then I was so interested in what she was doing, for she was washing with her own hands a set of China that is to be used during the General's visit, because it was given to Washington by the Society of Cincinnati. It has the Washington coat of arms on each piece, and a Latin motto beneath it. Then we got out and set on a side table a great China punch bowl that was presented to Washington by the officers of the French navy who came across the sea to aid in the Revolutionary War.

The silver tea-set that came from Mount Vernon is to be put on the sideboard tomorrow. Cousin Mary said that, so far as she could, she would use Mount Vernon things, as she felt sure that it would gratify General Lafayette.

But I must stop writing, for I believe that I can make myself useful. Cousin Mary had no special message to send. She is all absorbed in getting ready for her visitors.

By the way, mother, aren't we some distant connection to the Lees? It seems as if I had heard father say that he was a cousin once or twice removed; and I remember quite distinctly how badly he felt when Colonel Lee died. Mrs. Lee, as you know, lives in Alexandria, and her youngest son, Robert, seems on most familiar terms with all the family here. Mr. Custis treats him as if he were his son, which, by the way, he may yet become, if the boy and girl attachment between him and Mary goes on They are really quite devoted to each other.

I could fall in love with him myself, he is so

handsome and witty and gallant, but Cousin Mary has forbidden me even teasing Mary, saying that she doesn't want any such ideas put into the children's heads. But I just wonder how she is going to keep them out. She says that Robert is just like one of the family now, but as he goes to West Point next spring, he will doubtless grow away from them. But I can't help seeing that Cousin Mary and Mr. Custis have already adopted Robert Lee into their hearts, and would be nothing loath to have him marry Mary when the time comes; so if they go on falling in love, or rather keeping in love, their love story will run smooth. I wonder how it will be with mine, if I ever have one?

Love to Pater and the boys, and Mammy. with your own share always from your

VIRGINIA.

P. S.—It would seem as if this letter was long enough, without a postscript. But I want you to see to it that father writes to Captain Worth-

ington. He is so lazy, dear old soul, that he
will put the writing off on you. Don't let him
do it. Tell him how brave and handsome the
Captain is, and how highly he is esteemed.

III

Arlington, October 24, 1824.

Dear mother, and father, too; for this is for you both, as indeed, are all my letters. If you only knew all that I have to sacrifice in order to write, you would appreciate my letters. I have left the most interesting people down stairs. To be sure, they will not miss me—none, unless it is Captain Worthington. He, at least, says that he always misses me.

But first of all I want to tell you how glad I was to receive the home letters. And dear Pater; give him a kiss for me as a reward for the nice letter he sent to Captain Worthington. The Captain seemed so pleased; and he read every word of it to me, and I in return read him your letter. He was greatly interested, and said such lovely things about you, and what it must be to have such a home and mother. I suppose he feels it the more keenly because he has no home now. His adopted father and mother both died while he was at West Point, and he is quite alone with no near relatives.

About my clothes, mother; you need not worry at all. I asked Cousin Mary, and she says that they are quite fine enough for all occasions, even for the reception at the White House.

Yes, I read even that part of your letter to the Captain, and he said it did not matter what I wore, for I was always lovely. I told him that was the first silly remark I had heard him make; whereat he looked hurt.

But why am I running on in this way when you are impatient to hear all about the arrival of our distinguished guest? It was quite an imposing affair. I mean, of course, the arrival in Washington. We went over early and called at the White House. But Cousin Mary decided that we could see best from the carriage; so when word came that the party were about to enter the city, we drove to a position on the Avenue whence we could watch them pass.

A View from the Veranda of the White House
in 1814
showing the National Capitol

. . . . mother
. . ., and he

n need not
, and she says
all occasions,
White House.

A View from the Veranda of the White House
Lady return to . . . in 1814
and . . . showing the National Capitol
. . .

. . . way
. . . and
. . . quite a

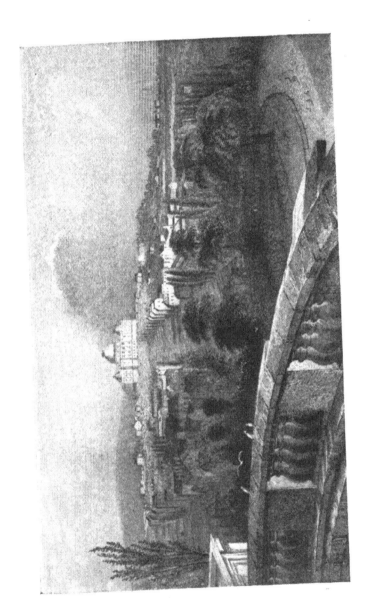

First came the band and some soldiers and naval officers; then, in an open carriage, the General, and with him the President, Mr. Adams and Mr. Custis. It was a beautiful day and the streets were full of people, who shouted and cheered all the way, and most of the time General Lafayette stood up in the carriage, bowing and smiling, and always with his right hand resting over his heart. He looked pleased and happy. His son rode on horseback beside the carriage, he on one side and Captain Worthington on the other. And—would you believe it? —the Captain saw us in all that crowd and gave us a bow and a smile.

We only stayed to see the procession pass an.i then came home, as Cousin Mary wished to be here to receive her guests. They drove up to the Capitol and then to the White House, where all the officials in Washington came to be presented to General Lafayette, and then they let the poor tired man drive over to Arlington, where he is to spend the next two weeks resting; so they say. But I wonder how much rest all these eager admirers and friends will allow him to take?

There are to be no receptions or dinners for a few days, but there is some one here nearly every hour of the day. The evenings are a little more quiet, and it is as good as reading history, and vastly more interesting, to hear the General tell his experiences when he first came to this country. How he does reverence and admire the great Washington!

We sat about the dinner table very late last evening, while Mr. Custis and he talked on and on about Mount Vernon, and I put my voice in once when I had better have kept silent. The General had asked after some of the old servants, and that led Mr. Custis to tell him that they were all free. He said that General Washington did not believe that slavery was right, and he well remembered hearing him discuss with the statesmen who visited at Mount Vernon the duty of emancipating all the slaves. Mr.

Custis ended by saying: " I shall follow his example. No black man will pass on as goods and chattels to my heirs."

Then poor, foolish me had to speak up and give father's views. And I bethought me of the sermon Dr. More gave us a few Sundays ago, when he proved so conclusively and beautifully that slavery was God's plan for the care of a weak and inferior race. You know we all thought it such a fine, clear argument, and father said it just expressed his views. Well, they listened politely to my little speech. Then Mr. Custis said : "Yes, I know Dr. More, and you can tell him for me that, the next time he preaches on slavery he had better let St. Paul furnish the text. I think he will find it in his letter to Philemon. "No longer a servant, but a brother beloved."

It was easy to see that no one endorsed Dr. More's views, and Captain Worthington really looked quite sad. So in future, your daughter will try to remember the old adage: "Silence is golden."

Sunday, the General felt that he must rest;
but as I had expressed a wish to attend a service in the old Rock Church, where you had
gone as a child, it was arranged for a party to go
on horseback. But when Sunday came Mary
had a headache, and George Lafayette decided
that he had best stay with his father. I was
greatly disappointed, until Captain Worthington
asked Cousin Mary if she would be willing to
trust me to his care. She gave a ready consent, and we started off in high spirits.

It is a long ride, but it did not seem so to
us, until we found ourselves late at the service.
But we had the ante-communion service and
the sermon, and we stayed afterwards to look
about the plain little church; and I had no
trouble in finding grandfather's pew, for the
little brass plate is still on the door. The out-
side of the church is so beautiful now, for it is
fairly embowered in ivy. We wandered about
the old graveyard, and I found the family vault.
It, too, is almost hidden by ivy, and I had to

lift the long trailing vines to read the inscription. Grandmother's name looks for all the world just as it does on the sampler that hangs in your room. When Captain Worthington read that grandfather was a soldier in the Revolutionary War and present at the surrender at Yorktown, he said: "You have something to be proud of."

We had a glorious ride home and a lunch all by ourselves, as the family and guests had all lunched and gone to their rooms, and we did not meet until dinner-time. We spent the evening together in the parlor. I played the harpsichord, and we all sang hymns for a while. And then we asked the General to tell us something about his own country, and he fairly made my blood run cold as he told of the horrors through which he and Madame Lafayette lived during those awful days of the French Revolution: and he expressed the profoundest gratitude to our government, and especially to President and Mrs. Monroe, for the efforts made in their behalf.

He said that Mrs. Monroe had saved his wife from the guillotine.

Although I had vowed to keep silence, I really could not refrain from asking him to tell us about his attempt to help the king and queen out of France. He gave a most graphic account of that fearful journey, and of how nearly it was accomplished when they were discovered and forced to return to Paris.

While the General was talking, Mr. Custis left the room, and, returning in a few moments, he laid two swords on Lafayette's knees, saying: "These are the swords I spoke to you about." The General at once rose to his feet, and holding a sword in each hand reverently kissed them. Then we all had the privilege of holding in our hands swords that had been carried by the great General Washington. One bore an inscription telling that it had been given to him by the Continental Congress.

I must not forget to tell you that the first thing General Lafayette noticed, as he came into the house on the day of his arrival, was the great lantern that hangs in the hall. He remembered having seen it at Mount Vernon when he visited there, and before he went to his room he walked up to one of the portraits of Washington, and stood for some moments regarding it with fixed attention.

Mr. Custis had had Peale's portrait of Washington hung in the General's room, an attention that seemed greatly to please him. I think his memory is wonderful, for he asked if the sideboard was not the one he had seen at Mount Vernon, and he greatly gratified Cousin Mary by noticing the china and silver and expressing his appreciation of having it used. Another attention shown the General is, that the chair set for him at the table is the one Washington always used at his own table in Mount Vernon.

But if I keep on writing all these little things I shall not have time left for the more important ones, and therefore much will have to wait until I am with you.

And now I must tell you about the interesting dinner party of last evening. O, if you could only have been here! President and Mrs. Monroe came over from Washington to what Cousin Mary called an informal dinner, and with them were Mr. and Mrs. John Quincy Adams. It was your daughter's rare good fortune to be one of the party that included such distinguished guests and I sat with ears wide open listening to what they had to say.

It seems that General Lafayette has had a long and intimate acquaintance with both the President and Mr. Adams. The General and Mr. Monroe are about the same age, and they were officers together during the Revolutionary War. Then the President was United States minister to France during those terrible days of the French revolution, and the General feels that the efforts made by him saved both his own and his wife's life.

And just here I must not forget to tell you of a most thrilling scene. When Mrs. Monroe came into the drawing room last evening, General

Lafayette went forward to meet her, and dropping on his knees he kissed her hand, and with tears streaming down his cheeks said: "Do I indeed see her whose brave courage saved my beloved wife from the horrors of the guillotine? Madame, my gratitude, my worship is yours."

Mrs. Monroe was much overcome, and everyone had to wipe away tears, for it was all so intense and affecting.

When the General had regained his composure, he gave us a vivid account of the visit Mrs. Monroe had made to Madame Lafayette when she was in prison at La Force, France. The day of her execution had been decided upon, and Mrs. Monroe arrived only an hour or two before the time set to conduct her to the guillotine. But she came surrounded by all the pomp and ceremony her husband could command, and in the name of the government of the United States she pleaded for the life and liberty of the prisoner. To her great delight, the request was granted, and liberty took the place of the guillotine.

Mrs. Monroe is very modest and retiring in her manners; but when the ladies were alone together for a time after dinner, both she and Mrs. Adams told us much that was interesting about their life abroad. Only to think of being the wife of a man who has been ambassador to England, France and Spain, then Secretary of State, and now President of the United States. Mrs. Adams has almost an equal claim to honor, for her husband has been minister to England and Russia, and is now President Monroe's Secretary of State; and Mr. Custis says that he will be the next President.

I wish I had time to tell you of a most interesting and exciting account that Mrs. Adams gave us of a journey from St. Petersburg to Paris, just after the fall of Napoleon Bonaparte. The carriage in which she and her young children took the long journey was stopped over and over again, and they were in great peril.

But I have wandered away from the dinner-table around which sat such distinguished guests.

[58]

How fine it would be if one could have all that was said there written down! There were so many reminiscences of the war; indeed, of two wars, and of diplomatic life in Paris and London. But I must tell you of one quite exciting little incident. The dinner was over but we ladies lingered, as General Lafayette was telling the story of the discovery of Benedict Arnold's plot to turn over the forts at West Point to the British. It seems that he was with Washington that morning, and witnessed all the excitement. He said that he should never forget the expression of sorrow and consternation on General Washington's face when he realized that Arnold was beyond question a traitor. And with quivering voice he said: "Whom, whom can we trust?"

At this point Mr. Adams spoke, saying in his slow, impressive way: "Yes, our country has already had two great traitors, Benedict Arnold and Aaron Burr." I happened to be looking straight in General Lafayette's face as Mr. Adams spoke, and I was startled to see his emotion. He flushed scarlet, and springing from his seat, he lifted his right hand as if taking an oath, and said: "Sir, Aaron Burr is more than a traitor. He is a murderer, who lives to-day unpunished. Alexander Hamilton was my first friend in America. He spoke my language; he understood my motive in coming; he took me to General Washington. I owe everything to him. I loved him as a brother. He should be alive today, enjoying the highest honor this country has to bestow. But Aaron Burr killed him."

In the silence that followed this outburst, Cousin Mary made the move for the ladies to go into the parlor. I was so curious to know what happened after we left that I questioned Captain Worthington, and was surprised to find that Aaron Burr's name affected him as intensely as it did General Lafayette. He could not talk about him, but said that some day he would tell me the fearful trouble Burr had brought to his family. And now, I remember that father can never hear Aaron Burr's name spoken without saying some bitter words about him. It must be some punishment to have to live on in a world where so many people detest you.

But I must not write a word more, for Captain Worthington has been sitting here for over an hour, waiting with Job-like patience for me to finish this letter, and go with him for a horseback ride. We manage to have a ride almost every day. So adieu.   Lovingly, your

VIRGINIA.

IV

Arlington, October 16, 1824.

Dear Mother:—Cousin Mary says that the family will be bankrupted by the postage on my big packages of letters. Has Pater made any complaints? I am glad the postage is due at the other end, and can only hope that you will feel that the letters are worth what they cost you.

You said in your last letter that I must tell you everything that happened. I can't do that, and I have just given up trying. I have not written for several days, for every hour of time has been taken up. There are so many people coming and going all the time, and I try to be some help to Cousin Mary. The weather is still glorious, and I have had a fine ride on my favorite horse almost every day. That reminds me, for he is always my companion on these excursions, of something Captain Worthington said the other day. I had been telling him what a dear, unselfish mother you were, and how grateful I was for the privilege of being here, although I knew that you were the one who should be enjoying it all, when he said: "Your gratitude can hardly be equal to mine."

"And pray, why are you grateful?" I asked. I looked at him as I asked this question, and the look in his eyes made me blush scarlet. But only because I am a silly girl. You remember, mother, how easily I do blush anyway. And there was really nothing to blush for, as he said at once, "You see I need a companion for my horseback rides; and what could I have done if you had stayed at Wyndham?"

"Taken Mary with you," I said. Whereat he shook his head and said, "No, not when young Lee is about. I don't care to cross swords with him."

But, dear me! why am I writing all this when I have three great occasions to tell you about. The first is the reception at the White House, when I wore my rosebud silk, grandmother's pearls and your white plumes: two things that you have often told me you wore at President Washington's reception in New York City.

Cousin Mary said I could tell you that I did the family credit, and General Lafayette kissed my hand and said that I was "resplendent;" while Captain Worthington said I was "a vision," and made him think of Wordsworth's lines:

> "She was a phantom of delight,
> When first she dawned upon my sight."

The President didn't say anything about me, but he asked after you and father, which showed that he remembered who I was, even in that crowd.

But I must begin in a rational manner and tell you all about the reception. Cousin Mary and the four gentlemen went to the White House to dinner, so Mary and I had to drive over alone. We went early, and were down stairs

... grandmother's
... two things that
... wore at President
... New York City.
... that I ...
... Lafayette kissed
... I was "resplendent,"
... I was "a ...

"General Lafayette kissed my hand."

... was a ... delight,
... my slant."

... first ... not say anything about me,
... asked ... rather, which showed
... who I was, even in that
...

... begin in a rational manner and
... at the reception. Cousin Mary
... gentlemen went to the White
... dinner, so Mary and I had to ...
... We went early, and were dressed ...

before the party came in from the dining room. At first it was quite informal. Mrs. Monroe welcomed us, and then asked Mrs. Adams, who was one of the dinner guests, to show us the great east room, that was to be opened that evening for the first time, the furniture having just arrived from Paris. It is very beautiful with carving, and every chair, sofa and table has a brass eagle on it. The great mirrors at each end of the room and over the mantels reflected the light of the innumerable candles, so that it was a most attractive place. Mr. Adams followed us into the room; and, as he looked about, he said: "This is where my mother used to hang her washing."

Mrs. Adams left us to take her place beside Mrs. Monroe in the blue parlor, and very soon all the rooms were crowded, for there was a perfect rush of the people who wished to meet General Lafayette. He stood near the President, and gave everyone a pleasant smile. Sometimes he recognized an old friend, and then he would try to detain him for a little conversation, which was usually cut short by the crowd pushing on.

Mr. Custis said that I must be sure to remember to tell father that I shook hands with Mr. Calhoun, the Secretary of War, and with Mr. Clay, the Speaker of the House of Representatives. Then there was a man with a big head and piercing black eyes whom I did not .meet, but as he seemed to always have a crowd about him I asked who he was, and Captain Worthington seemed proud to ·tell me that it was Daniel Webster of Massachusetts, a wonderful orator.

I suppose that I ought to tell you, mother, about the dresses. Some of them were very beautiful. Almost everybody wore silk or satin, and one or two had velvet gowns. Both Mrs. Monroe and Mrs. Adams wore the handsome white satin dresses in which—so Cousin Mary told me—they had been presented at court.

But if I write another word about the reception, there will not be time to tell you about the great event of the week, which was a visit to Mount Vernon.

There had been a good deal of talking and planning for this visit. But at first I had no idea that I should be one of the party, and I am quite sure that I owe this great treat to Captain Worthington. He has confessed to me that he told the General of my great desire to see Mount Vernon. At any rate, General Lafayette especially invited Mary and me to go with him. Mr. Custis objected a little, but yielded when the General said: "I want them them to go. They will remember it long after you and I are gone." Wasn't it nice of him?

We started about ten o'clock, going to Washington in carriages, and when we came to the river I found that I was to have the novel experience of a journey in a boat propelled by steam. I felt timid at first, but when Captain Worthington assured me that there was no danger, I quite enjoyed the trip, we went so rapidly.

There was quite a party on board. The President could not go, but he sent the Secretary of War and Mr. Adams to represent him, and Mr. Clay and a number of other invited guests made up quite a distinguished party.

At Mount Vernon the boat anchored in the river, while we were taken ashore in small boats. Mr. Lewis and a number of gentlemen received the party and conducted us up the hill to the mansion.

You have been there, so you know what a beautiful place it is, but I don't think it compares with Arlington, either in size or stately grandeur.

General Lafayette was very much overcome as he entered the house, and he said to Mr. Custis: "Can it be that I am here in the home of the greatest and best of men, my paternal friend? Forty years ago he was here to welcome and embrace me, and now I can only visit his tomb."

We went first into the little parlor, where

Mr. Custis told us his sister Nellie used to enter-
tain her friends, and where she often delighted
her adopted father by playing on the harpsichord
that he had given her.

General Lafayette had asked that he should
be permitted to visit the tomb of his illustrious
friend before the lunch that had been prepared for
the party was served.

So, after a few moments' rest, we all walked
down the hill to the tomb.

The caskets within were covered with flowers,
and the doors stood partly open. But no one
went within except General Lafayette. He knelt
and kissed the casket that held the body of his
friend, and came out to us with tears streaming
down his face.

Then Mr. Custis stepped to his side and
taking his hand, placed upon one of his fingers
a heavy gold ring that encased some of the hair
of the great Washington; and, still holding his
hand, he said:

"My dear and honored friend, take this gift

as a memento of him whom the whole world
honors as the greatest of patriots; but whom we
knew as the noblest, truest and best of
friends."

Mr. Custis' voice faltered more than once,
and tears ran down his cheeks as he spoke.

General Lafayette was very much overcome.
He kissed the ring and pressed it against his
heart, then he embraced Mr. Custis and thanked
him in broken words for his "precious, precious
gift."

Everybody shed tears, and not a word was
spoken until we again entered the house. Then
Mr. Lewis conducted the General to his room,
while the rest of us walked about the grounds, and
for your sake I went all over Mrs. Washington's
garden, that is so attractive with its box-
bordered beds of flowers.

The lunch was served in the great banqueting
hall that Washington added to the mansion after
he became President, and General Lafayette entertained us with an account of his helping to

put the first paper on the wall so that it might be ready for the ball given in his honor, He grew very animated and happy as he talked of his visit of forty years ago.

We had quite a little excitement on our way to the boat. The horses on the carriage that took the General down the hill became frightened at the noise of the cannon that was being fired as a parting salute, and they made a mad rush that threatened to overturn the carriage; which doubtless would have happened if Captain Worthington had not dashed forward and, grasping the bridles, held and turned them aside from the steep bank.

I don't just like to tell you what your brave daughter did, but when I saw Captain Worthington hanging to the horses heads as they plunged madly down the road, I just fainted dead away, causing another excitement. I was very much ashamed of myself, but just one awful thought came to me, and then I did not know anything more.

Well, everybody was very kind, and General Lafayette came and sat beside me on the boat and said: "I am much flattered and exalted that my young friend loves me so well that my danger made her heart stop beating."

Captain Worthington was devoted to me all the way, and as everyone else seemed to think that I must be kept quiet, we had a delightful time all by ourselves.

It was dark when we reached Arlington, and Cousin Mary sent me at once to my room for a good rest before the late dinner. When I came down stairs every one was so tender and solicitous about my health that I felt that I was of great importance.

The talk that evening was all about Mount Vernon, and so much was told that I must remember and tell you when I see you. But you will be especially interested in what we did Sunday, for we all attended service in Christ's Church, Alexandria, and sat together in the Washington pew. Mr. Custis and George Lafa-

yette wanted to do it in memory of their youth-
ful days, and General Lafayette said that he
must go and pray in his honored friend's
church.

We had to make an early start, the carriage
taking the General and his son, and Mr. Custis
and Cousin Mary, while Captain Worthington,
Mary and I rode on horse-back. Robert Lee
came out to meet us, and we all rode up to the
church and entered while they were reading the
Psalter, causing no little commotion as we filed
in the great square pew.

I ought to have been very much impressed by
the grand company and the memorable associations of the place, but some way I could not
help thinking more of the coming separation
from all these delightful friends than of the fact
that I was sitting in the seat where the great
General and first President had so often wor-
shiped God.

After the service, everyone, from the rector
and wardens down to the sexton, pressed about

General Lafayette, eager to take his hand and hear him speak.

From the church, the party in the carriage drove to Mrs. Lee's, while the rest of us, including young Robert, rode back to Arlington.

At Sunday evening dinner Mr. Custis entertained us by telling about some of the pranks he used to indulge in when a boy at Mount Vernon, and especially at the time when he and George Lafayette were there together, He said that they were always taken to church every Sunday morning, but were never allowed to sit side by side, Mrs. Washington taking charge of young Lafayette, while the General saw to it that his restless grandson sat quietly in his seat. He said that General Washington always stood during the prayers, and he stood beside him, while his grandmother knelt devoutly, and she saw to it that the young Lafayette kept on his knees.

I wonder if all these reminiscences interest you as they did me. I never tire of hearing

Mr. Custis tell of his boyhood days at Mount Vernon.

But, alas! it is all coming to an end. Only a few days more, and they will all leave Arlington and start out on a tour through the States that will take many months.

I heard General Lafayette tell Mr. Custis how pleased he was with Captain Worthington, and that he was to have him during all of his stay in America.

The Captain does not look as happy as he ought to over his fine prospects. He always seems sad when he speaks of leaving Arlington.

He told me the other day that the last two weeks had been the happiest of his life. I don't wonder at it, for it is such a lovely spot and I have been so happy here myself, that I fear that life will seem empty and vacant when it is all over.

Captain Worthington says that he must surely see Wyndham some day, and that comforts me a little. But good-night and good-bye.

It will not be long until I shall be with you. Love to Pater and the boys. Tell Mammy that I am not forgetting her, and that Chrissie is getting anxious to get home.

Ever your own.

VIRGINIA.

CHAPTER V

Arlington, October 20, 1824.

This letter, mother dear, will be quite unlike any that I have written you, and you will be greatly surprised over what I have to tell.

I don't know where to begin or what to say; it is all so new and strange, and wonderfully delightful and beautiful. I am so dazed that I can't remember when I wrote you last.

But never mind. I will just tell you of yesterday, for that is the day that will forever stand out from all the others; the day when I wakened up to the knowledge that I am blessed among women; that I am rich and happy in the love of the noblest of men. It seems so strange that he should care for me, and how can I ever return this beautiful love and devotion?

I wonder if I can make you understand all that happened yesterday. Captain Worthington

says that he felt in honor bound not to tell me
of his love, until he had an answer to the letter
that he wrote father several days ago.

There! That reminds me that this letter will
not be such a surprise to you after all, for that
letter must have reached father, and also one
from Cousin Mary that Harry tells me he asked
her to write in his behalf. So you and father
know all about the great gift that has come
to your daughter, and it only remains for me to
tell you how I came to find out about it before
the time.

Yesterday—yes, it was only yesterday—although it seems much longer; General Lafayette
and his son went over to Washington to spend
the day with the President. So Captain Worthington was left free, so he said, to devote himself
to me, and of course, we went for a ride in the
park. It was another of those perfect autumn
days that have followed each other all this glorious month. Cousin Mary came out to see us
mount and start off, saying that she envied us

the joy of riding under the grand old trees that are now brilliant with their autumn tints. We did exclaim a good deal at first over the charm of it all, but we soon grew quiet and subdued, for we knew that it was likely to be our last ride together. And the Captain talked a good deal about his plans for the future, when his duties as aide to General Lafayette would be ended, and he told me that he should take advantage of his first leave of absence to visit Wyndham.

We took a long ride, and as Captain Worthington assisted me to dismount at the great block in front of the mansion, he said: "Whenever you are at leisure, you will find me in the little writing-room."

This little room has been our favorite place of meeting whenever we wished to enjoy a quiet talk together. I always write my letters here, and it has grown to be the dearest place in the house to me. I found Cousin Mary busy giving out stores to the servants, and Mary deep in her morning lessons. So I was not long in find-

ing my way to the dear little room. As I
entered, Captain Worthington said: "Excuse
me for a few moments, for I am putting the fin-
ishing touches to a little memento of our visit,
that Mr. Custis has given me permission to
trace on this window."

I wonder if I have told you that one of the
Captain's accomplishments is tracing on glass.
He has made some lovely things for me.

My curiosity led me at once to the window,
where, to my surprise, I found a delicate and
beautifully carved picture of two rings interlocked together, and he was cutting a wee
initial within each ring. It needed only a
glance to show me that one was that old ring of
grandmother's that I always wear, and the other
a small diamond ring that the Captain has told
me was very precious to him because it had belonged to his own mother.

I said, "That is beautifully done. But what
a queer fancy to carve them there. Why have
you done it?"

... the dear little room. As I
... Washington said: "Excuse
... for I am putting the fin-
... to a little memento of our visit,
... given me permission to
...

... I have told you that one of the
... accomplishments is tracing on glass.
... lovely things for me.

... me at once to the window,
... to my surprise. I found a delicate and
... carved picture of two rings inter-
... together, and he was cutting a tree
... each ring. It needed only a
... to see that one was that old ring of
... that I always wear, and the other
a small diamond ring that the Captain has told
me was very precious to him because it had belonged to his own mother.

I said, "That is beautifully done. But what
a queer fancy to carve them there. Why have
you done it?"

He did not answer me in words, but simply turned and looked into my eyes, for I was standing close beside him, and then something wonderful happened, for, like a sudden flash, everything was made clear and I felt a great wave of joy sweeping over me. My eyes must have spoken for me, for his face became as radiant as my own, and he bent over and kissed me. So, without a spoken word, we came to know that we belonged to each other.

After a while we had a long, quiet talk, and Harry (he is not to be Captain Worthington to me any longer) told me of his letter to father, and that he had felt that he ought not to speak to me until the answer came.

I said, "You did not speak, you only looked; and in some way the look told me everything."

I found that he had talked with Cousin Mary and had her approval; so now we only wait for the letter from home, which is sure to add your consent and blessing to our already full cup of joy.

[81]

O, mother, you will be delighted with Harry. He is so noble and good and kind, and father will find such satisfaction in his high ideals, his lofty patriotism and his good common sense. He looks at everything just in the right way. Only think what a help he can be to my brothers. His influence will always be on the side of all that is good and true.

He is an ideal soldier, and I must tell you a secret, that Cousin Mary said I was not to tell any one; but you and father now have a right to know it. The Secretary of War told Mr. Custis the other day, that a promotion to the head of a regiment would be given Captain Worthington as soon as his duty as aide to General Lafayette was over. But I am not going to write any more until the home letters come. Harry has to go to Baltimore on business for the General tomorrow. He says that he will hurry back as fast as a swift horse can bring him, but I am to open and read father's letter if it comes, as it surely will, while he is away.

Now, there is just one thing more that I must tell you. We had fully resolved, before we left this little room, yesterday, that no word was to be said to the friends until after the home letters came. We felt that it was due to you and father, so we decided to act just as if nothing happened. And I am sure I tried to, but when I went into Cousin Mary's room to ask her something about my dress, she looked at me and said: "Why Virginia?" And then she put her arms about me and told me how pleased she was over my happiness, and by dinner time everyone in the house had loaded us with congratulations. General Lafayette kissed me, and called me "a blessed woman." Still, mother, there is nothing settled. No promises will be given until we have your and father's approval.

Your happy, happy,
VIRGINIA.

[83]

VI

Arlington, October 23, 1824.

Dear Mother:— I am writing because Cousin Mary has made me realize that you will be feeling troubled and anxious. Still, I do not believe that my letter will bring you relief. I never could keep anything from you, and if I write you will know how crushed and broken-hearted I am. Only think! Three days ago I wrote you such a happy letter, and now all the joy in my heart has been killed by father's letter. It came only a few hours after Harry had started for Baltimore, and I brought it up here that I might read it in this little room that is now so full of tender associations. I read it over twice before I could take in its full meaning. And when I did realize it I must have fainted, for Cousin Mary found me lying on the floor, with the open letter in my hand. She was so alarmed lest something awful had happened at home that she read the letter. Then she had me carried to my bed; and O, she has been so tender and kind and so wise in her advice.

I suppose that father did not mean to be cruel, and he had no idea that I would ever see the letter; for he not only withheld his consent, but he forbade Harry speaking to me of his love. But you see it all turned out so different; and the one thing I am thankful for is, that the letter came while Harry was away; for he must never know how I have suffered; and by the time he comes I shall, with Cousin Mary's help, he able to meet him calmly, and prepare him for what he has to endure before he sees father's letter.

When you receive my happy letter; the last bright, joyful letter you will ever receive from your heart-broken daughter, you will understand; and you can make father comprehend that in any case I would have had to know about his letter.

[85]

How cruel, and bitterly hard it all seems!
How can father look at it as he does? Surely he
loves you and can realize how desolate life would
be without you. And yet he seemed to think
nothing of asking Harry to put me quite out
of his life.

Of course, I have long known that there had
been a tragedy in our family; for you had to
tell me in order to explain some things that
father did and said. And oh! I felt so sorry
for him. But I thought it was all a thing
of the past, and never dreamed that its dark
shadow would cloud my life. I cannot believe
that it is right, but I know father too well to
have any hope that he will ever see it in any
other light.

But, mother, you will believe that Harry is
everything that is noble, and I shall love him
always. Poor mother! You will have a sad
time trying to believe that father is doing
right, while your heart is full of sorrow for
me. I can't write any more now. Don't worry.

I am going to be brave and strong, and I will write again as soon as I have seen and talked with Harry. I cannot bring myself to send any message to father, but you will doubtless let him read this letter. O! mother, I wish you were here. I need you. Still it helps me to know that you love me. And even if my heart is too heavy for me to know the joy of having such a mother, yet I am your own loving daughter.

VIRGINIA.

VII

Arlington, October 25, 1824.

Dear Mother:—Your sweet letter has helped us both very much. I prize it most of all for the comfort it has given Harry. He has been so self-contained, brave and manly, that if it were possible, I love him more than before this trouble came upon us. He needs comfort, for he has the bitterness of feeling that his own father's acts brought this sore trouble to us. Yes, it must be true, although I never believed it before, that the sins of a father are visited upon his children. But was this a sin? Doesn't father think it all right to fight a duel?

Harry doesn't think that any circumstances justify one man in killing another. But I remember hearing father say that only by holding a man's life of less value than his honor, could society be kept up to a high standard. Doubtless he would have counselled Uncle Thomas to accept Major Wood's challenge; and then, when it ended in the awful tragedy of the death of both, why should he lay the penalty on an innocent child, whom it made fatherless and motherless; for the shock and grief killed Harry's mother.

I would lay all the blame on that wicked, scheming Aaron Burr; for Harry tells me that he drew them both into one of his deep, iniquitous schemes for gaining political power; and then, to still better work out his evil purposes, he filled Uncle Thomas's mind with false accusations against Harry's father, so that he was moved to write Major Wood an insulting letter that called forth the challenge to the duel.

Harry understands all about it. For although it was kept from him until he was twenty-one years old, his uncle then told him the whole story of the terrible tragedy that had made him an orphan. But, as he never saw any one connected with it; never heard it alluded to,

save in that one confidential talk with the
uncle who had been a real father to him, and
whose name he bears; it grew to be only a dim,
half-defined horror, from the memory of which
he always tried to escape.

But when he wrote to father, he felt that
he ought to tell the story of his father's death,
and of his adoption by his uncle. I asked him
if the name of Colton did not suggest the tragedy. But he said "No," for his uncle had
purposely withheld the name so sadly associated with his father.

Harry seems able to enter into father's feelings far better than I can. He says that he
can understand the shock his letter must have
given, and that he does not wonder that father
shrinks with horror from even the thought of
giving his only daughter to the son of the
man whose hand brought upon him the bitterest
sorrow of his life; while to me it looks like an
even thing—the wrong as deep and terrible on
one side as on the other. Why not let our love
bridge the chasm?

But I know father too well to have any hope. I know how strong his prejudices are, and that he can hate as intensely as he can love. There is nothing for us but broken hearts and divided lives.

O, mother! mother! why did it have to be? It breaks my heart anew each time I realize that you are never to know Harry. For to know him would be to love and admire his noble, unselfish character. Oh, if only you could hear him plead with me to be patient and forgiving with father! But he does not understand father as I do, and I know that he is indulging in the hope that the letters sent from here, and especially that of General Lafayette, will make father see it all in a different light. But I know that there is no hope. Only, mother dear, I am sure you feel for and with us, and if it were in your power to do it, you would sweep all this misery away.

I have not yet told you how Harry received the news. He came into this little room the day he returned from Baltimore, looking so handsome and happy, and one glance at my face told him that something was wrong, and then, instead of living up to my high resolves, I just lay in his arms and sobbed. And when he begged to know why I was so heart-broken, I gave him father's letter; and oh, mother, how it would have touched your heart, if you could have seen the anguish in his white, drawn face. It was a long time before either of us could say a word.

Harry was the first to regain command of his voice, and then, very quietly and calmly, he told me what he knew about his own father's death and that made it all clear. And I did forget myself in sympathy with him. And I even offered to give you up for his sake.

But he at once said: "No, Virginia, I will not tempt you to be unfaithful to your father and mother. We must wait and hope for some other way out of our sore troubles."

But there, I hear him coming up the stairs,

and this is our last day together. I will leave
my letter until the parting is over.

Only a day since I left this letter. But it
seems like a life-time, for I have said good-bye
to Harry. The party all left this morning, and
Mr. Custis went with them. So the two cous-
ins and I are quite alone. Cousin Mary has
been so good to your poor child. She tries to
keep me with her all the time. But I told her
that I must finish this letter to you. I don't
think I will write another letter while I am
here. There will be nothing to tell, for everything has come to an end. I hope Cæsar will
be here in a day or two, for I want to go home.
I want to see you. Sometimes it seems as if
I were turned to stone, and did not care for
anything. But I do long for you, mother dear.
I shall not try to tell you much about this last
day. Only I do want you to know how good
General Lafayette was to me. He asked me
to take a little walk with him down to the

spring, and as soon as we started he began to talk about Harry. I shall treasure always the lovely things he said, for he seems to admire and love him almost as if he were his own son.

Then he talked to me about his wife; told me of her wonderful courage and cheerfulness during those awful days and long, weary months that they spent together in that fearful prison at Olmutz. Then, turning suddenly, he took both of my hands in his and looking into my eyes, he said: "And you, my dear young lady, must learn to be like my noble wife if you would be worthy of my brave friend."

I think his words inspired me with courage, for I was able to stand with the family and watch the party start off this morning. Of course, Harry and I had had our own leave-taking up here in this little room, but that is something I can't write about.

There were a good many people to see them off, and I am sure that in all the excitement no one noticed me, and I saw little save Harry's pale, calm face; and I know it pleased him that I was there and could control myself.

General Lafayette, too, looked his approval, and as he bent to kiss my hand at parting, he whispered just two words: "Be brave!"

I watched them until the winding road was lost to sight under the great trees. Just at the last turn, Harry faced his horse about, lifted his hat and waved it. I hope he saw that I was standing just where he left me. And so it is all over.

I asked Harry to write to me, but he said that not even for me could he do a dishonorable thing; and it would be dishonorable to do so when father had so positively forbidden his even telling of his love. And when I pleaded for just one letter, he said: "'I could not love thee, dear, so much, loved I not honor more.'"

I shall go back to you, mother, no longer your gay, light-hearted girl. I am years and years older than when I left you.

It will be hard to say good-bye to Cousin Mary. She has been so good, and I have come to love her dearly. I wonder if I will ever feel like coming here again. General Lafayette is coming back to Washington before he sails for home, and he told me that I must surely be here to meet him. But, of course, that cannot be.

O, mother! mother! why must that dreadful past mar my life? But I am forgetting General Lafayette's farewell words, and I must remember to "be brave." I will try not to distress you any more. So good-bye until I see you. And be sure that nothing can make me other than your devoted and loving daughter.

VIRGINIA.

———

It is evident that Virginia Colton kept to her resolve of not writing again, for the letter of October twenty-fifth was the last one in the package marked:

> "My daughter Virginia's letters from
> Arlington House, October, 1824."

But you will remember that the secret com-

ARLINGTON HOUSE

As it is to-day

Virginia.

partment of the old desk held a package of letters written nearly a year later, and two of
these will give the always-to-be-desired happy
ending to this little old-time love story.

VIII

Arlington, September 1, 1825.

Dear Mother—Can you imagine my feelings as I sit here in this dear little room, and realize all that has come to pass since I sent you my last wild, despairing letter from here last autumn?

I wonder sometimes if it can all be true, or if I have simply passed from a horrid nightmare into a lovely dream.

But, thank God! it is all a blessed reality. When father bade me good-bye, he told me that the past was to be very truly a dead past to us both; that we must try to put away even the memory of the dark cloud that had come between us.

Don't think for one moment that I fail to appreciate all that he has given up. He had much to overcome, and he has been just splendid in the way he has done it. It is simply wonderful. I suppose that fearful sickness of mine did it. You have told me that even a heart of stone could not have resisted the incessant pleadings of my wild delirium.

O, what a coming back that was to life and reason, with life made so beautiful! It was all sunshine, and how rapidly I grew well and strong. I can never forget the joy Harry's first letter brought to me, for then I learned how grandly generous father had been.

But here I am, writing all this out of the fulness of my happy heart, and forgetting in my selfish joy that you are looking for a report of the journey here.

But there really isn't a thing to tell; or rather, it is all swallowed up and lost in the one all-important event of the meeting with Harry. And where do you think we met? Why! on the very spot where he came to my aid last year. It isn't a full year, and yet it seems a life-time.

I had my face close to the window of the

641431 A

carriage watching for the spot; when, to my great surprise and joy, I saw Harry standing by the roadside, and Peter beside him holding the bridles of two saddle-horses.

Could anything have been arranged lovelier than that we should ride to Arlington just as we did last year? Harry was beside the carriage as it stopped, and I ready to spring out, and—well—I suppose Cæsar will describe the meeting to you, so I need not try.

Harry's joy was subdued and solemn. He said that it seemed almost as if I had been given back to him from the dead. And I could not keep back the tears, but they were tears of joy.

But we both grew very light-hearted and gay as we rode on together, and talked over all that had happened since the sad day of our hopeless parting. And then of the future—our future together! It was all so lovely and full of brightness, like the dawn of a beautiful new day.

We reached Arlington just at sunset, and

such a welcome as they gave us! Even the dogs knew me and barked joyfully.

Cousin Mary is the same dear, kind soul as of old, and Mary has grown more woman-like and lovely. Mr. Custis seemed so glad to see us, and congratulations were quite the order of the day.

General Lafayette is the guest of President Adams at the White House, so I shall not see him until tomorrow. I feel as if I could hardly wait a day for his greeting and good wishes.

Harry has told me of his gleeful reception of the news that father had given his consent to our engagement, and I just wonder how he will receive me.

We had a quiet little dinner last evening, and even Harry endorsed Cousin Mary's command that I should go early to bed.

Harry has his headquarters in Washington, in order to be near the General. But Cousin Mary had a room ready for him, so he stayed here last night and we had a fine ride right after breakfast. Then he went over to Washington.

Cousin Mary plans to take me this afternoon for the call on General Lafayette. I will write again in a day or two; but I know that you will be satisfied with the word that I am well and happy. That word happy does not seem big enough or strong enough to hold or tell all that I feel. Joy is a better word, isn't it?

But good-bye for this time, with my best love for Pater and the boys and your own dear self.

VIRGINIA.

P. S.—True to my habit, I must add a postscript. You will remember my telling you about the linked rings that Harry carved on one of the windows of this, our little room Well, when we came in here last evening, the light of a full moon falling through the glass caused them to sparkle as if really set with jewels, and when I remembered all they stood for to Harry and me, I could not resist going up and kissing the glass; whereat Harry said: "Don't waste kisses on cold glass." And he didn't.

As we stood there looking out at the beautiful moon, it seemed as if it really were our honeymoon. At any rate, all things beautiful and bright have come to us.

IX

Arlington, September 5, 1824.

Dear Mother—Your letter with its good news from home came this evening, and Harry and I enjoyed it together. He has already quite adopted himself into the family, and always speaks of you as "mother."

I am so sure of his place in your heart, and you will, I know, be greatly interested in the all-absorbing news that I have to give to you; which is nothing less than that Harry has received his commission as colonel, and with it orders to report for duty at West Point, as soon as General Lafayette sails for France.

It is a great honor for so young a man to be appointed instructor in tactics at West Point, and Harry says that he owes it all to General Lafayette; while Mr. Custis remarked that it required brains to teach tactics, and that the Secretary of War was very careful in his selection of instructors for the young soldiers; which remark I accepted as a compliment to Harry, although he is too modest to see it in that light.

But the most wonderful part remains still to be told. Yesterday the President sent for Harry to come to his private office; and when he obeyed the order he found General Lafayette and the Secretary of War closeted with the President. Mr. Adams at first questioned Harry as to his knowledge of tactics and his ability to speak the French language. The last question the General answered for him, saying: "I assure your Excellency he talks quite like a Frenchman."

Well, the result of the conference was that the President told Harry to prepare himself, while at West Point, for a trip abroad, as, in deference to the request of General Lafayette, it had been decided to send him to Paris next June, where he was to spend six months studying the tactics of the French army.

Of course this is not official, and all I am writing you is to be for some time a family secret. But only think, mother dear, this means that I am to realize my dream of going abroad, for you and father will surely give your consent to our marriage in June. It is all so wonderful that I still feel as if I were in dreamland.

But I must tell you about my visit with the General, who seems to be our good providence. We went over to the White House Wednesday morning and after a wait of a few moments in the blue parlor, a message came from Mrs. Adams asking Cousin Mary to come to her room, as she was suffering from one of her headaches. So I was left to receive General Lafayette alone. And such a welcome as he gave me! He fairly overwhelmed me with compliments and congratulations. And he was so excited that he mixed his French and English in a manner that taxed my wits to fully understand.

But it was good to see him and hear him talk about Harry. He said that his one disappointment was that he could not stay in America long enough to be a guest at our wedding. "But," he said, "you are coming to France and we will make that one grand occasion."

Then he told me that he was going to send me something to wear on my wedding day—something very precious, because it had been his dear wife's—a pearl necklace that he had given her soon after their marriage. And he said it was always to remind me of one of the bravest and best of women.

While the General was talking President Adams came into the room. Everyone says he is cold and distant in his manner. But I did not find him so at all, and he quite won my heart by telling me that he considered Harry one of the most promising young officers in the army—one whose future was likely to reflect credit both on himself and on his country.

Don't such words from the President of the United States make you feel proud, mother? The President asked the General if he would spare me for a brief call upon his wife in her room, and he himself went with me.

I found Mrs. Adams as lovely as ever; and she, too, had so many kind words to say, and showed such genuine interest in our plans and hopes.

But I cannot tell you more of this visit now, for I am all impatient to write you of our plans for next June.

Harry spent last evening here, and we talked everything over with Cousin Mary and Mr. Custis. By the way, they are both coming to Wyndham for the wedding, and I have asked Mary to be my bridesmaid of honor, and Harry is going to invite young Robert Lee to stand with her. That will make Mary happy and please all the family.

We have everything beautifully planned, but it is all conditioned on your approval, and we have until next June to talk it all over and make and change our plans. But it all seems simply perfect to me.

What do you think Mr. Custis did last evening? He asked me to go into the dining room with him, and then he took from the sideboard a lovely old-fashioned silver teapot, and after telling me how often he had seen his grandmother pour tea from it, he said: "And it is to be yours as a reminder of all that has come to you in Arlington."

Only think of your little daughter Virginia, falling heir to Martha Washington's silver teapot and Madame Lafayette's pearl necklace, and having before her the prospect of a wedding journey to Paris, and a visit in the home of that grand and noble friend of our country and our special friend, General Lafayette.

Surely, "To him that hath shall be given." For all this is coming to me because I am to be the wife of one of the best and noblest of men.

I long to have you as proud of Harry as I am, and that, too, is coming in the happy years before us, when you and father will learn to lean upon and trust him as your son.

Tell dear old Mammy about the June wedding. She has always said that June was my lucky month.

Chrissie is holding her head very high, for she, too, expects to go to Paris.

Love to Pater and the boys and a heart-full for your own dear self, from your happy, happy daughter,

VIRGINIA.

n 2 l9886